THE LITTLE CHRISTMAS ACTIVITY BOOK

by Luna
Anna Pomaska

DOVER Luna
PUBLICATIONS, INC
New York

Published in Canada by General Publishing Company, Ltd.,
30 Lesmill Road, Don Mills, Toronto, Ontario.
Published in the United Kingdom by Constable and Company, Ltd.,
3 The Lanchesters, 162–164 Fulham Palace Road, London W6 9ER.

The Little Christmas Activity Book is a new work, first
published by Dover Publications, Inc., in 1988.

International Standard Book Number: 0-486-25679-0

Manufactured in the United States of America
Dover Publications, Inc.
31 East 2nd Street
Mineola, N.Y. 11501

NOTE

With this book, you can enjoy the charms of Christmas while teasing your brain. These fun and simple puzzles and mazes are all illustrated, and include instructions and solutions (the solutions begin on page 54). Solving these puzzles will keep good boys and girls busy and in the holiday spirit. You will learn to count and spell, follow the dots, search for hidden images, find differences and even read picture stories. And of course the drawings—of angels, reindeer, toys, Santa Claus and other Christmasy things—can all be colored in. These fun activities will complete your holiday frolicking.

It's Christmas Eve and Santa Claus is delivering his presents. But it is not always easy for him to find his way to children's houses. Help Santa get to this house.

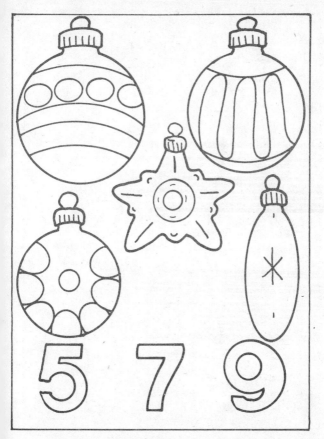

Count the Christmas ornaments on this page and circle the number you have counted.

Bobby knows Christmas is a time for giving. Here he is visiting Susan with a present. But something looks funny. Can you find five things wrong with this picture?

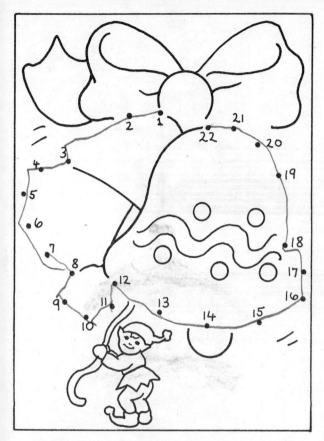

What is this little elf doing? Connect the numbered dots to find out.

H	O	U	S	E	B
A	N	G	E	L	A
E	O	A	C	J	L
E	L	F	G	K	L

BALL

Look at the pictures and their names on the opposite page. Now find the names hidden in the box above and circle them. "BALL" is an example.

HOUSE

ELF

ANGEL

The pictures of Santa's little helper on these two pages may look the same at first, but there are five differences. Can you find them?

Judy is having so much fun making Christmas cards she doesn't notice the six letters hidden around her. Help her find the letters E, J, m, n, o, and w.

START →

END •

These children are sledding to Grandmother's house to bring her presents. Help them stay on course.

13

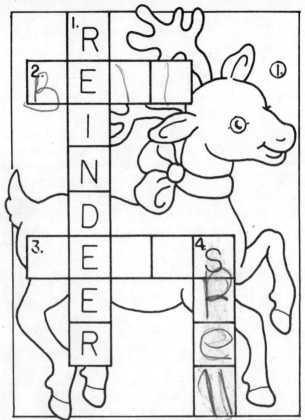

To complete the crossword puzzle, spell out the names of the three pictures on the opposite page. The number next to each picture tells you where its name belongs on the crossword grid. "REINDEER" is an example.

14

There is a winter picture hidden here. To make it appear, color the shapes marked "B" blue, the shape marked "G" green, the shape marked "O" orange, and the shapes marked "Y" yellow.

16

Mr. and Mrs. Claus PICTURE STORY

Mrs. Claus put a [gift]

under the [tree] 4

[Santa]. The [tag: TO: SANTA] read,

[pen] 4 [bee] 4

Here is a Christmas story that uses pictures for some of the words or parts of words. Can you figure out the meanings?

Christmas!" "O m [eye] w [hat] [can] it [bee] ?", said [Santa].

He O/ed it and found a w [foot],

long  .

said, "thank U !

know Y

it was 2

O/ed 4

Christmas! It will keep me n[ice] and [toast]y in m[eye] [sleigh] Christmas night."

END.

Santa Claus is carrying gifts in his sack, but he is also bringing some hidden things. Can you find a feather, a fish, a rabbit and two birds?

21

Count the angels on these two pages and circle the number you have counted.

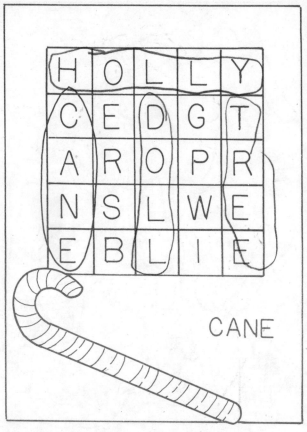

H	O	L	L	Y
C	E	D	G	T
A	R	O	P	R
N	S	L	W	E
E	B	L	I	E

CANE

Look at the pictures and their names on the opposite page. Now find the names hidden in the box above and circle them. "CANE" is an example.

HOLLY

DOLL

TREE

25

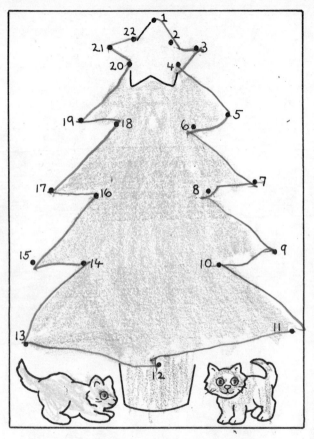

Connect the numbered dots to see what the kittens are playing under.

These children are singing Christmas carols. Help them find their way to each of the four houses in order.

These two pictures of Alice sleeping on Christmas Eve appear to be the same, but they are not. Can you find the five differences?

To complete the crossword puzzle, spell out the names of the three pictures on the opposite page. The number next to each picture tells you where its name belongs on the crossword grid. "ANGEL" is an example.

The children are hanging up their Christmas stockings, but something seems strange. Do you notice five things wrong with this picture?

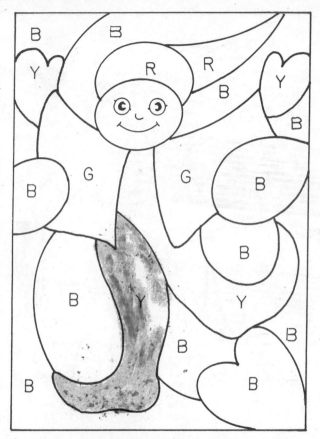

Here is a hidden Christmas picture. To see who is here, color the shapes marked "B" blue, the shapes marked "G" green, the shapes marked "R" red, and the shapes marked "Y" yellow.

This little helper is so busy getting the reindeer ready for their Christmas Eve flight he doesn't notice the five hidden objects. Can you find a bell, a bird, a fish, a mouse and a seal?

Dorothy has been a good girl this year. Now she is writing her Christmas list to Santa Claus. Help her remember all the toys that begin with the letter "D" by going through only their pictures on the way to the mailbox.

Count Santa's reindeer on these two pages and circle the number you have counted.

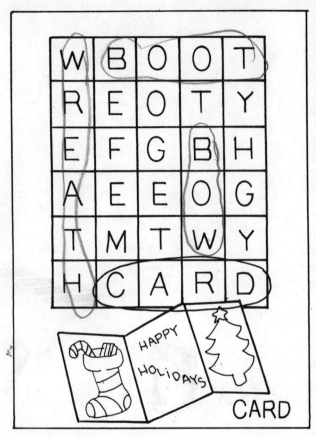

W	B	O	O	T
R	E	O	T	Y
E	F	G	B	H
A	E	E	O	G
T	M	T	W	Y
H	C	A	R	D

CARD

Look at the pictures and their names on the opposite page. Now find the names hidden in the box above and circle them. "CARD" is an example.

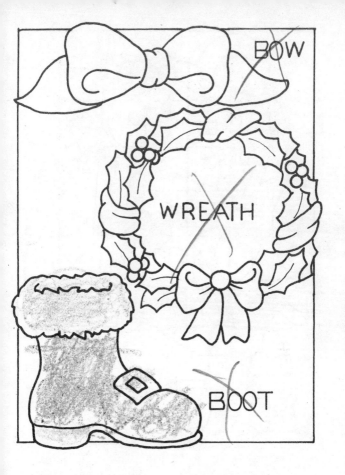

BOW

WREATH

BOOT

Lisa and John are having so much fun building their snowman Frosty they don't notice the letters hidden on them and around them. Do you see the letters C, E, H, i, N, o, S, T (two of them), w, and X?

A CHRISTMAS PICTURE STORY

TABBY 👃 when

Christmas is n👂.

The 👦👧👦 hang up their 🧦

Here is a Christmas story that uses pictures for some of the words or parts of words. Can you figure out the meanings?

and every 1 is

wrapping .

are

singing in front

of TABBY's .

TABBY likes 2 sit

under the 🎄

2 look at the 🔔.

The night 🐝 4

Christmas **TABBY**

sleeps next 2 the

and waits

4 2

visit and bring him

a little . end

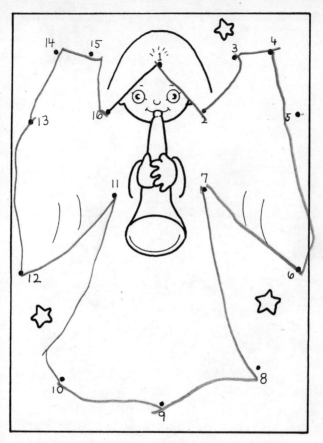

Connect the numbered dots to make this heavenly musician appear.

The pictures of a Christmas tree on these two pages may look the same at first, but they are different. Do you see the five differences?

To complete the crossword puzzle, spell out the names of the three pictures on the opposite page. The number next to each picture tells you where its name belongs on the crossword grid. "COOKIE" is an example.

Janet and Tommy are having a Christmas party, but something seems strange. Can you find six things wrong with this picture?

Connect the dots to see what has been left on the table for Santa Claus to enjoy on Christmas Eve.

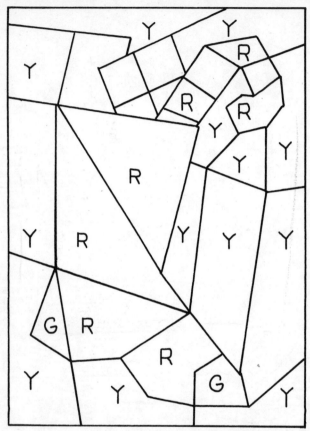

There is a Christmas picture hidden here. To see it, color the shapes marked "G" green, the shapes marked "R" red, and the shapes marked "Y" yellow.

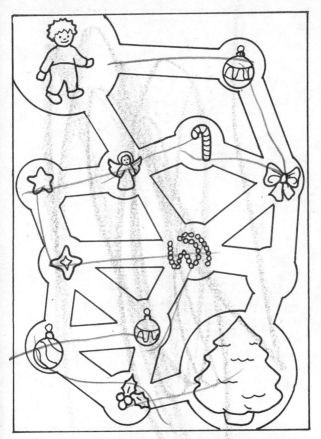

Joshua wants to decorate the Christmas tree. For him to do so, he must gather all of the ornaments without passing over the same path twice. Can you help him?

SOLUTIONS

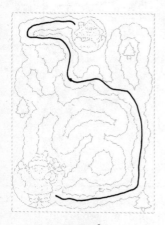

page 4

page 5

page 6

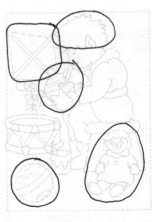

page 7

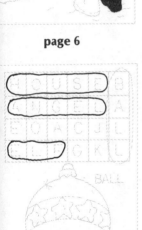

page 8

page 11

page 12

page 13

page 14

Mr and Mrs. Claus
PICTURE STORY

put a **gift** under the **Christmas tree** for [4].

The **tag** read **Santa open before** [4]

page 17

Christmas!" "O **my** [eye] **what can** it **be**?" said **Santa** He **opened** it and found a w **warm**

page 18

long **scarf** **Santa** said," thank **you**! [eye] I know **why** it was **2 be opened before**

page 19

Christmas! It will keep me **nice** and **toasty** in **my** [eye] **sleigh** Christmas night."

page 20

page 21

pages 22 and 23

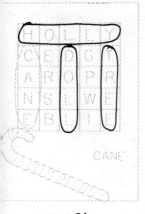

page 24

page 26

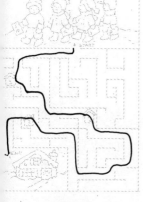

page 27

page 29

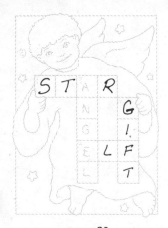

page 30

page 32

page 34

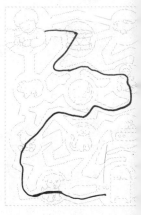

page 35

pages 36 and 37

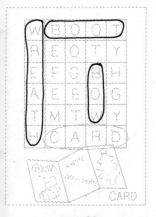

page 38

page 40

A CHRISTMAS PICTURE STORY

Tabby knows when Christmas is near The children hang up their stockings

page 41

and every one is wrapping presents (or gifts) Carolers are singing in front of Tabby's house

page 42

Tabby likes to sit under the Christmas tree to look at the ornaments The night before Christmas Tabby

page 43

sleeps next to the fireplace and waits for Santa to visit and bring him a little mouse end

page 44

page 45

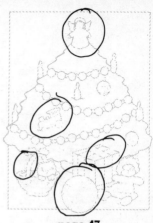

page 47

page 48

page 50

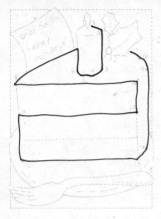

page 51

page 53